Children

by
Gail Saunders-Smith

Pebble Books

an imprint of Capstone Press

Pebble Books

Pebble Books are published by Capstone Press
151 Good Counsel Drive, P.O. Box 669, Mankato, Minnesota 56002
http://www.capstone-press.com

2 3 4 5 6 05 04 03 02 01

Library of Congress Cataloging-in-Publication Data
Saunders-Smith, Gail.
    Children / by Gail Saunders-Smith.
    p. cm.
    Includes bibliographical references and index.
Summary: In simple text and photographs, describes the accomplishments of a child
growing from a baby to a toddler and finally a young child.
    ISBN 156065-491-0
    1. Child development—Juvenile literature. 2. Children—Juvenile literature.
[1. Growth.] I. Title.
HQ767.9.S277 1997
305.231—dc21   97-23587
                                                       CIP
                                                       AC

Editorial Credits
Lois Wallentine, editor; James Franklin, designer; Michelle L. Norstad,
    photo researcher

Photo Credits
FPG/Barbara Peacock, 8; Jim Cummins, 14; David Waldorf, 16; Cheryl Maeder, 18;
    Arthur Tilley, 20
George White Location Photography, cover
Unicorn Stock/Tom McCarthy, 4, 6
Valan Photos/V. Wilkinson, 10; Ian Davis-Young, 1, 12

Table of Contents

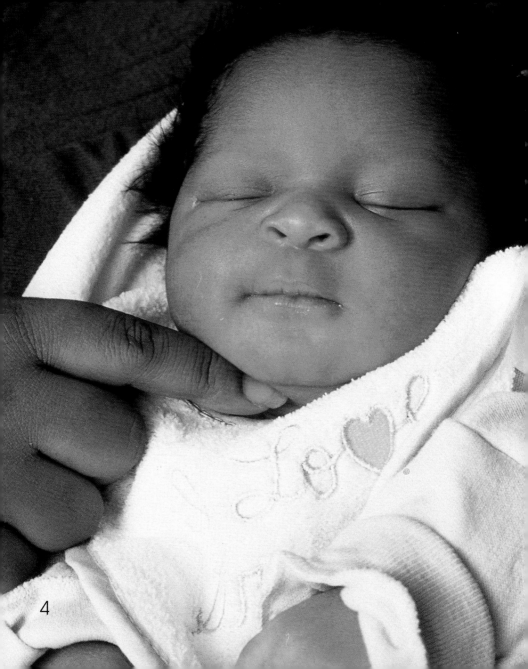

4

Look at this baby sleep.

Look at this baby eat.

Look at this toddler walk.

Look at this toddler talk.

Look at this toddler work.

14

Look at this child ride.

Look at this child hit.

18

Look at this child play.

Look at this child tie.

Words to Know

baby—a person who was just born

child—a young person

hit—to smack or strike at something

play—to take part in a game or an activity

ride—to travel on a vehicle or animal

sleep—to rest deeply

tie—to make a knot or bow with two pieces of string

toddler—a young person who has just learned to walk

walk—to move along on one's feet

work—to do something using one's energy or ability

Read More

Marzollo, Jean. *How Kids Grow.* New York: Scholastic, 1998.

Simon, Norma. *All Kinds of Children.* Morton Grove, Ill.: Albert Whitman, 1999.

Internet Sites

Julia's Rainbow Corner
http://www.juliasrainbowcorner.com

Kid's Corner
http://kids.ot.com

Kid's Korner
http://www.kidskorner.net/main.html

Note to Parents and Teachers

This book describes the physical growth and learning progression from babyhood to toddlerhood and into childhood. These concepts provide opportunities for reflection. The clear photographs support the beginning reader in making and maintaining the meaning of the text. The noun is repeated several times before a change. The verb change in each sentence is clearly depicted in the photos. Children may need assistance in using the Table of Contents, Words to Know, Internet Sites and Index/Word List sections in this book.

Index/Word List

Word Count: 45
Early-Intervention Level: 4